10 minutes of Praise using the Names of God

by Michelle Holstein

Scripture quotations used in this book are from The King James Version of the Bible (KJV).

First Printing, 2019
ISBN 978-1-6466-9100-5

Printed in the United States of America

Dedication

This is dedicated to my sister, JoDi, a believer with deep faith. I made a format of worship without thee's and thou's for her with scripture verses to support the name entries. My sister, Moni, beautifully and graciously helped format this. Thanks to my family, many cousins, especially Chuck & Ruth Anholt and Linda Lindsey, as well as my daughter, Amy, who checked the Bible verses. The Anholts prayed for me through this project. This book cover was designed by my nephew, Kevin Trigueiro. Many thanks to Suzanne Levy and several others who edited, encouraged, and prayed for me through this project!

Contents

Introduction

God has fearfully and wonderfully made us as Psalm 139:14 says. The brain is a wonderful gift given to us by our Creator. We have a responsibility before God to use our brain properly. Another Scripture verse tells us about our heart. "For as he thinketh in his heart, so is he. . ." (Proverbs 23:7) What we think about, we will become. As we meditate on God then we will know Him. "That I may know him, and the power of his resurrection, ..." (Philippians 3:10)

If someone tried to describe me to you, they might say, "Her name is Michelle. She has a nickname, Mici, and some people call her Mrs. Holstein. She is a wife, a mother, a daughter, a sister, a believer, and a friend." Then they might describe my characteristics. "She is passionate about life and she hates sin in her life. She loves her immediate and extended family." Those names and characteristics begin to describe me. The more names and descriptions of me given, the better I am known. As we focus on God, we will get to know Him better. We can spend ten minutes in the morning focusing on who He is, and His character, and as we know Him more, we will hunger for His goodness. The joy of the Lord will fill our hearts.

To maintain daily peace we must start the day focusing our hearts on God by giving Him praise. All creation praises God. Somehow each part of creation gives praise unto His Creator. One day as I played praise songs on the piano early in the morning, I noticed birds singing around my windows. At day break, the birds sang along with the harmonious song of the praise. The birds are not afraid to sing their praises.

We start a time of worship by remembering His works and thanking Him for them. In our walk in Christ, we can be thankful to God for the following things:

- He has taken our place of sin and shame.
- He has begotten us unto a living hope by the resurrection of Jesus Christ from the dead as we willingly turned in repentance and faith to the Lord Jesus Christ.
- He has shown us in His Word the expression of God's will for our daily lives.
- He loves us and nothing can separate us from His love.
- He has filled us with all spiritual blessings in heavenly places in Christ Jesus.

The goal is to *enter* into a time of praise. Throughout the day we may have to return to that place of refuge for renewed peace. This time of praise will allow your brain to respond obediently to the promptings of the Holy Spirit throughout the day. Our Father encourages us in Scripture to focus on Him and His works." O give thanks unto the LORD, for he is good: for his mercy endureth for ever. ... Oh that men would praise the LORD for his goodness, and for his wonderful works to the children of men! For he satisfieth the longing soul, and filleth the hungry soul with goodness." (Psalm 107: 1, 8, 9)

Once Jesus Christ became real to me I collected many names of God and His character qualities. I began to learn these names of the Lord and focused on them almost every morning. I put the names and character traits on 3x5 cards and scratch paper, keeping them bound in a rubber band and tucked in with my Bible. Then I organized this list because I didn't want to lose the precious names of God I had found. They were like a gold mine to me. When I read my Bible, it seemed the Holy Spirit would point out new names of God. Sometimes I heard others pray and sing names of God in meaningful ways which I had never heard before. It is beyond my comprehension how great is the name of our Living God and how impossible to ever adequately describe Him. At the end of this book is the list I have collected and used for the specific purpose of lifting up the name of God. This list has

Biblical names and common names that refer to one or all parts of the Triune God. I've found that it has worked for me.

I wanted God's presence but I didn't always know how to start in worship, seeking His presence. I thought to myself, "Well, if I say the names back to Him, then maybe my heart could become prepared." I know that to learn a person's name, I should repeat the person's name back to him in sentences, with his name used several times, varying its usage. For instance, if I had just met my husband, John, for the first time, I would use his name John in several sentences. I would say, "Hi, John. How are you doing today, John?" A little later I might say something about his car, "You have a beautiful 2003 white Mustang, John."

After that conversation, I would remember his name much better because I had repeated it several times in a row. Why would I remember it? I would remember it because of repetition of his name. After doing that, it would be easier to remember John's name, and John would become a better acquaintance of mine. Why would I want to remember his name? I want to get closer to him and one way of getting closer is to never forget his name. John would also like it if I remembered that He had a special car.

This is true with God, also. The more I remember His names, the more I feel better acquainted with God. Having a deeper relationship with Him and remembering His names enhances that relationship. It pleases God that I remember His name. So, I began following a pattern of praise and thanksgiving back to God. My 'Michelle Moments' with the Lord, early in the mornings, became precious. ". . . all the upright in heart shall glory." (Psalm 64:10) " . . . He was extolled with my tongue." (Psalm 66:17)

After I read the names of God and His characteristics out loud before the Lord, I felt so enriched and it seemed like the

Holy Spirit's presence was clearly there with me. I wanted His very close presence in my life and I have continued to seek Him daily in praise. This method also cleared my brain as I placed Jesus as the center of my life each day. I was able to go out of my house with peace, joy, and a desire to encourage others. "When righteous men do rejoice there is great glory. . ." (Proverbs 28:12) Great glory was felt in His presence—His heavy dignity. I chose a couple of the pages of the names of God that I had on my list and lifted praises to God by using those names. "Enter into his gates with thanksgiving, and into his courts with praise; be thankful unto him, and bless his name." (Psalm 100:4) I began by thanking Him for my blessings and then I moved into praising Him. This is an example of how I began.

Dear Heavenly Father, I love You and I come to You in praise and thanksgiving. Thank You for my salvation. Thank You for taking my place and suffering for my sins. Your Name Is High and Lifted Up. You Are the Hope of the Nations, You Are My Hope, You Are My Strong Defense, You Are the Rock that Is Higher than I, You Are My Refuge, You Are My Strength, and You Are Everything to Me. You Set the Prisoners Free. You Are A Father to the Fatherless, A Light House, My Shield, My Defense. You Are My Hope. You Are My Strength in Times of Trouble. You Are Word of God Incarnate. You Are the Lord of Hosts, The Creator Of The Ends Of The Earth, The Beginning And The Ending, You Are My All in All, The Lamb Of God, Crown Of Glory, The Diadem Of Beauty, The Spirit Of Judgment. You Are My Gracious Providence, The Rock Of Israel, The Saving Strength Of His Right Hand, The King Of All The Earth, A Refuge For The Oppressed, A Refuge In Times Of Trouble, The Shadow Of His Wings, My Stay, The Great High Priest That Is Passed Into The Heavens. You Are Jesus, The Son Of God.

You Are The Same And Your Years Have No End, Lord Jesus.

Here is a practical approach for anyone to use in their daily time to praise God or 'glory' in Him. I use the paperclip approach in my Praise Section. The paperclip is put on that Day's List of the Names of God. I move it over to the next Day's List when I am done praising Him. That way, I have not lost my place for the following day. After I have spent time in worship, I write down five names in my journal that ministered life to me during that time of worship. This is the question I ask myself: How did God reveal Himself to me today? I look up the Bible verses for each entry. I try to recall those names of God throughout the day. Here is an actual daily journal entry:

8/23/19: <u>How did God reveal Himself to me today?</u>
1. Perfector of My Faith, Psalm 138:8
2. Perfect Sacrifice, Hebrews 9:26
3. Power is Limitless, Psalm 62:11, Romans 8:11, Ephesians 1:19-20, John 10:17-18
4. Quiet Rest, Matthew 11:28
5. Sanctifier, Psalm 8:4, Philippians 1:6 & 2:13, Acts 17:280

I also write the names and the Bible references on a 3 X 5 card. (You probably could put it in your phone like a grocery list.) I take the 3 X 5 card with me to bed so that I can meditate on God's names at night before I sleep. This is a practical approach for anyone, and yet you can add your own personality to your time of praise. After spending time in worship by naming His names which are listed by days in "15 Minutes of Praise" and then writing in both my journal and on a 3" x 5" card five of the names which especially minister to me, I can easily recall them later. The truths become reinforced in my heart each day. When I hear these names of God, I remember a little. When I hear the names and I write them down, I remember more. When I see the names, repeat them, hear them, and write them down, then I remember so many more truths about God. The goal is to see the Names of God imbedded in my heart, so when I enter into a time of prayer and/or praise, I can work in cooperation with the Holy Spirit to enter into His presence. My hope is that through "15 Minutes of Praise" the Bride of Christ will move closer into the presence of the Bridegroom. "Because he hath set his love upon me, therefore will I deliver him: I will set him on high, because he hath known my name." (Psalm 91:14)

Once you have completed the lists, you may begin the lists again. I sent these lists to my sister, to whom this book was dedicated, and within a few days, she sent me more names of God. I expect the same will happen to everyone who applies this in their lives. You will find more names of God. On <u>Day 14</u> you will find a culmination of verses that describe the manifold beauty and goodness of God.

As the Bride of Christ we should prepare our hearts to shine with His love each day, until the day we see Him face to face. Yes, it will be a wonderful day when the Body of Christ meets our Savior. "I will greatly rejoice in the LORD, my soul shall be joyful in my God; for he hath clothed me with the garments of salvation, he hath covered me with the robe of righteousness, as a bridegroom decketh himself with ornaments, and as a bride adorneth herself with her jewels." (Isaiah 61:10) We need to keep Him on the throne of our heart each day until the time of His second coming.

We need to make sure that we don't take for granted the great works of God in our lives. We must remember to praise God as the Samaritan leper did. He cried in desperation to Jesus and His cries were answered. "And one of them, when he saw that he was healed, turned back, and with a loud voice glorified God, And fell down on his face at his feet, giving him thanks: and he was a Samaritan. And Jesus answering said, Were there not ten cleansed? but where are the nine? There are not found that returned to give glory to God, save this stranger. And he said unto him, Arise, go thy way: thy faith hath made thee whole." (Luke 17: 15-19)

We must remember to give glory to God for the good works He has done and will do for us. We must always give thanks and praise to God for His goodness to us before and after answering our prayer. He is worthy. It is important to thank God for food, clothing, shelter, family, love, and purpose. This is a good way to begin our attitude of praise. Anyone can do this. "Enter into his gates with thanksgiving . . ." (Psalm 100:4) It's very simple.

Ascribing splendor and majesty to God is to glory in God. To glory is also used as a verb, as in 'to glory in something'. The glory of God's presence was found in a tangible way with the children of Israel. They could sense His heavy dignity. "It came even to pass, as the trumpeters and singers were as one, to make one sound to be heard in praising and thanking the LORD; and when they lifted up their voice with the trumpets and cymbals and instruments of music, and praised the LORD, saying, For he is good; for his mercy endureth for ever: that then the house was filled with a cloud, even the house of the LORD; So that the priests could not stand to minister by reason of the cloud: for the glory of the LORD had filled the house of God." (2 Chron. 5:13-14)

God's glory filled the newly constructed temple. This was tangibly experienced by those around, who saw a cloud fill the temple. His *presence* was felt. He, the Great I Am, was pleased to cause His glory to dwell in the temple. We are now the living Tabernacle of God where His Divine Presence dwells. "To the end that my glory may sing praise to thee, and not be silent. O Lord, my God, I will give thanks unto thee forever." (Psalm 30:12) We have the Secret of His Tabernacle, His Spirit in us. ". . . in the secret of his tabernacle shall he hide me." (Psalm 27:5) We live in the Secret of His Presence by having His presence inside of us. "Thou shalt hide them in the secret of thy presence" (Psalm 31:20)

Will we let this secret presence of God grow inside of us? The early believers gathered together and became a corporate group called 'the people of God'. "But ye are a chosen generation, a royal priesthood, an holy nation, a peculiar people; that ye should shew forth the praises of him who hath called you out of darkness into his marvellous light; Which in time past were not a people, but are now the people of God: which had not obtained mercy, but now have obtained mercy." (1 Peter 2:9-10) This corporate group of people was meant to give purposeful praises to Him who called them out of darkness.

"They looked unto him, and were lightened:
and their faces were not ashamed." (Psalm 34:5)

They were able to look to Him and their faces were lightened because they had dealt with the sin issues in their hearts. They were at peace with both God and man.

One day while praising God, suddenly the Spirit of God said, "You have something to straighten out." I had forgotten some money I owed the church audio department. I got up and went to the church to pay the $16. I was holding back something I owed to someone. If we want a sweet relationship with the Holy Spirit, then all our relationships with man should be right. We should be at peace with all men. Then I asked God if there was anything else in my heart that He needed to show me. The principle of forgiveness is a 'Kingdom of Light 'principle. God did show me where I had been harboring a level of unforgiveness in my heart which I hadn't realized before. When he showed me, I asked for forgiveness for harboring unforgiveness. "If I regard iniquity in my heart, the LORD will not hear me:" (Psalm 66:18)

Until we can get these relationships right with man, our relationship with God is affected, and the Holy Spirit is grieved. You will not feel the presence of God when the Holy Spirit is grieved. If you can picture a cross, you can see the symbol of our love relationship with God. The vertical of the cross reminds us of our relationship with God and the horizontal of the cross reminds us of our relationships with man. "Looking diligently lest any man fail of the grace of God; lest any root of bitterness springing up trouble you, and thereby many be defiled;" (Hebrews 12:15) Where unforgiveness resides, there also resides a root of bitterness in our hearts. It sours our relationship with God, making it difficult to feel His Divine Presence. "To whom ye forgive any thing, I forgive also: for if I forgave any thing, to whom I forgave it, for your sakes forgave I it in the person of Christ; Lest Satan should get an advantage of us: for we are not ignorant of his devices." (2 Corinthians 2:10-11)

If we allow unforgiveness, Paul said, we have given Satan an advantage. One of the definitions of the word "advantage" is a wrestling term. When we don't forgive, Satan can get the advantage over us. Satan wrestles with our soul and gains an advantage when we don't forgive. I don't want anything or anyone to interrupt my relationship with God or grieve the Holy Spirit. This Kingdom of God is an Everlasting Kingdom. We have been translated into the Kingdom of Light and are no longer part of the Kingdom of Darkness. The Kingdom of Light operates under principles of forgiveness, love, and light. "That ye would walk worthy of God, who hath called you unto his kingdom and glory." (1 Thessalonians 2:12)

Each night before I go to bed, I have to put a lubricant in my left eye because some tear ducts in it were damaged twenty years ago. Sometimes I do not place enough of the lubricant in my eye, and when I wake up, my eye cannot open without severe pain. When this happens, blinking and looking at light hurts terribly. One day I had a "Michelle Moment". Ouch!!! I woke up and couldn't open my eye because my eye had swelled from not enough lubricant. It was my daughter's birthday and I couldn't even text her, 'Happy Birthday'. Somehow, I had to get my eyes open so I could get the lubricant in. You know, that's hard to do in the dark, and it was painful to open my eye. In a half an hour's time, little by little, I was able to slip more ointment into my eye so that I could blink. Then my eye could receive the light, again. I had to stay in the dark while I went through this process. I could not turn the light on and get on with my day. My eye was painfully bruised and light just caused more pain.

I prayed and asked the Lord to take the swelling down in my eye. It was then that the Lord showed me that bitterness and unforgiveness is just like this. By not putting enough lubricant in my eye at night, or in spiritual terms, not getting my heart right, it leaves my spiritual eye painfully sore, not able to receive the Light of Christ. It stops the light of God's presence from coming into my time of worship. When I ask the healing oil of Jesus to cover my heart's bruise, by asking for forgiveness, I can see the Light again. "I counsel thee to buy of me gold tried in the fire, that thou mayest be rich; and white raiment, that thou mayest be clothed, and that the shame of thy nakedness do not appear; and anoint thine eyes with eyesalve, that thou mayest see." (Revelation 3:18)

My uncle advised me at my wedding to 'never let the sun go down on your anger'. Always kiss and makeup before you lay your head on your pillow. This attitude is a soothing ointment to your marriage, and it actually helps in all your relationships. The lubricant of forgiveness will soothe your spiritual eyes, bringing the Light of Jesus Christ back into your life.

> *Only God can turn*
> *a mess into a message,*
> *a test into a testimony,*
> *a trial into a triumph, and*
> *a victim into a victory.*

We have to be careful that no root of bitterness starts growing in us. Many people can be affected by our bitterness. It troubles ourselves and others around us by our unforgiving heart. "The spirit of a man will sustain his infirmity; but a wounded spirit who can bear?" (Proverbs 18:14) What man can live prosperously with a wounded spirit? An unforgiving spirit increases the pain in a contaminated spiritual heart.

Allowing God to remove bitterness from our hearts will bring revival inside of us. Bitterness interrupts the sweetness of worship. Unforgiveness is like a low-level fever. It weakens us and we can't hear or feel God. When we operate in unforgiveness, the bitterness that follows causes us to operate in the flesh. God's powerful grace can be used to reconcile ourselves to one another and to Him. The Great Forgiver lives inside of us. Using this acronym shows the *GRACE* at work:

> *God's*
> *Riches*
> *At*
> *Christ's*
> *Expense*

There is nothing that we have done that we didn't receive forgiveness for at salvation. We must do the same for others. The only way to get freedom is to let bitterness go. To receive freedom in worship, people who have hurt you need to be forgiven. You find freedom when you forgive, and you can feel God's presence in worship. "And when ye stand praying, forgive, if ye have ought against any: that your Father also which is in heaven may forgive you your trespasses." (Mark 11:25) If you haven't forgiven, you haven't gone low enough in humility. Humility is not thinking less of you. It is thinking of you less. You will never leave where you are, until you decide where you would rather be. As for me, I would rather be close to the Lord, feeling His presence. Applying this principle of forgiveness at all times will bring His presence, and staying in forgiveness will allow you to stay in that place of rest. We should show forth His praises by worshipping Him with the awe and respect He deserves. We are a part of His Marvelous Light now. We have an amazing Everlasting King of this Kingdom of Light.

". . . whereby we may serve God acceptably with   reverence

19

God wants to make His presence known to us in our lives. Through a time of praise with a clean heart, we can sense His Divine Presence and glory. His presence settled in the temple with His heavy dignity. We have the same Living God of the Old Testament, but He dwells in us now.

Jesus taught us to pray by praying in Matthew 6. He said, "Our Father, which art in heaven, Hallowed be thy name." If Jesus gloried in God by saying, "Hallowed be thy name", then we should, too.

I have developed this plan for two weeks of worship for ten minutes a day. You may not experience any emotion when you do this, although I do get emotional. There are two parts to our brain, one for feelings (which express our emotional barometer) and one from the objective part (from which words come). At times, the words from our brain may not adequately express what our heart wants to say. God gave us emotions to emphasize and add to our words. Sometimes we don't feel like praising God, but we praise Him because God is worthy. It is hard to praise the Lord with just words that would adequately describe our thoughts about Him. As we start using the terms in worship to describe God, then the emotions follow. God uses our emotions to help us better emphasize what we feel towards the Lord.

Many are not emotional about their faith and that's okay. This method can also be used to establish a time of praise to God if you do not want to get emotional. If we take approximately ten minutes daily, with a spirit of respect and awe to God, peace will be established in our hearts. The names of God are beautiful and it is a blessing to call Him who He is.

I begin my day by singing some simple songs about Him, about how I love Him or about His goodness. I sing from my heart to the Lord. I find it much easier to genuinely praise the Lord when I am alone, but this is not the only time that I lift up praises to Him. When I was younger and healthier I would lie on the floor and worship. Any way of worship is good: kneeling, walking around, standing, or sitting. Find a way of praise time that suits your personality. For instance, I have found that if I am going to face a certain direction, I like facing the east the best. "But as for me, I will come into thy house in the multitude of thy mercy: and in thy fear will I worship toward thy holy temple." (Psalm 5:7) "For as the lightning cometh out of the east, and shineth even unto the west, so shall also the coming of the son of man be." (Matthew 24:27) It is just a preference on my part. You may find your preferences as well. Just as God made each of us unique, He made our worship preferences unique. God bless you as you walk this journey. I hope you enjoy the following list as much as I have.

Descriptions of the names of God are capitalized for emphasis. The author's own interpretation as well as dictionary definitions are used. The Hebrew names for God are from: 1) the *Holy Bible*, Holman Bible Publisher, Copyright 1984, Crown Reference Edition, Marginal notes and 2) Thomas E. Ward, *The Names of God*, (Wilmington, DE: Partners in Ministry, 1995), Eric Celerier's email sent August, 2019, eric.celerier@jesus.net.

Adonai, (My Master and Lord, Complete submission to God, God is the possessor of me.), Genesis 15:1-2

Amnos or Amnion, (Lamb), John 1:29

Asah, (Maker), Isaiah 54:5

El-Chayim, (The Living God, God introduces Himself as the One who is Alive from all Eternity and for all Eternity. He is thus a God who acts practically, in every situation in daily life. God is not a theoretical God, but the God of life.), Joshua 3:10

El-Elyon, (The Most High), Genesis 14:18-20

Elohim, (A plural noun revealing God is a trinity), Genesis 1:1-2,

El-Olam, (The Everlasting God), Genesis 21:33

El-Roi, (The strong one who sees. God sees our troubles and He sees everything we do.), Genesis 16:13

El-Shaddai, (Almighty God, The Strength Giver and Satisfier of His People. By this name, God reveals Himself as the God who has all power in Heaven and on Earth.), Genesis 17:1, Genesis 28:3

Jehovah, (God is self existent.), Exodus 3:14-15

Jehovah-Jireh, (The LORD will provide.), Genesis 22:14

Jehovah-M'Kaddesh, (The LORD who sanctifies.), Leviticus 20:1-8

Jehovah-Nakah, (The LORD who smites.), Ezekiel 7:9

Jehovah-Nissi, (The LORD my banner or the Lord is My Banner. God introduces Himself here as the God of dignity, strength, courage, and involvement.), Exodus 17:3-16

Jehovah-Osenu, the Lord Our Maker, (This name of God affirms that the source of all life is in Him. He created all things and it is He who breathes life into everything.), Psalm 95:6

Jehovah-Rohi, (The Lord Is My Shepherd. The Lord presents Himself as a shepherd who has a close relationship with each sheep, knowing each one by its name and taking care of each in an individual way.), Psalm 23:1-3

Jehovah-Rophe, (The LORD that heals. Divine healing includes that of the soul and body.), Exodus 15: 25-26

Jehovah-Sabaoth, (The LORD of Host), Genesis 2:1

Jehovah-Shalom, (The Lord is Peace.), Judges 6:23, 24

Jehovah-Shammah, (God's presence is there or, the Lord Is There. This name emphasizes the omnipresence of God. God is present, always and everywhere. Nothing and no one can escape from His presence. Even if we run far away from Him, He is there.), Ezekiel 48:35

Jehova-Tsidkenu, (The LORD our righteousness), Jeremiah 23:5, 6

Orthrinos-Aster, (Morning Star), Revelation 22:16

Pele-Yaats, (Wonderful Counselor), Isaiah 9:6

Pistos, (Faithful), Revelation 19:11

Qadowsh-lysh, (Holy One), Isaiah 40:25

Qanna, (Jealous), Exodus 34:14

Semah, (Branch), Zechariah 6:12

Sur or Petra, (Rock), Psalm 18:46

Thura, (The Door), John 10:9

Yasha, (Saviour), Isaiah 43:11

Yeshua, (Jesus, the Lord is Salvation, is the name above all other names; the only name by which men can be saved. This name represents the last name of God in Biblical revelation. It expresses the Beginning and the Ending of everything. The coming of Christ represents the culminating point of the plan for humanity's salvation.), Matthew 1:21

A Bondman to My Lord, Genesis 44:33

A Broken Vessel, (A vessel, from Greek, means body, a broken body that perishes.), Psalm 31:12

A Bulwark that Never Fails, 1 Samuel 30:1-20, Isaiah 26:1

A Bundle of Myrrh, Song of Solomon 1:13

A Covert from the Tempest, (covert means shelter), Isaiah 32:2

A Fire, Jeremiah 23:29

A Friend that Sticks Closer than a Brother, Proverbs 18:24

A Gin and a Snare to the Inhabitants of Jerusalem, (Gin: a trap), Isaiah 8:14

A God in Israel, 1 Samuel 17:46

A God of Mercy That Endures Forever, Psalm 86:15, Deuteronomy 33:27

A Great King above All Gods, Psalm 95:3

A Great Light, Isaiah 9:2

A Hammer that Breaks up the Rock into Pieces, Jeremiah 23:29

A Hope Steadfast and Sure, Hebrews 6:19

A Judge Who Judges According to an Individual's Actions, 1 Peter 1:17

A King, Jeremiah 23:5

A Lamp for My Anointed, Psalm 132:17

A Light that Shines in a Dark Place, 2 Peter 1:19

A Light to Lighten the Gentiles and the Glory of Your People Israel, Luke 2:32

A Love that Is Never Failing, Hebrews 13:5

A Man Approved of God among Us by Miracles and Wonders and Signs, Acts 2:22

A Man of Sorrows, Isaiah 53:3

A Mighty Terrible One, Jeremiah 20:11

A Mystery of Godliness, 1 Timothy 3:16

A Nail in His Holy Place, (a pin that is a constant and sure abode), (*Holy Bible*, Holman Bible Publisher, Copyright 1985, Crown Reference Edition, marginal notes), Ezra 9:8

A Place of Broad Rivers and Streams, Isaiah 35:8

A Place of Refuge, Proverbs 14:26, Isaiah 4:6

A Polished Shaft, (A smooth, sharpened arrow, see Hosea 6:5, Jesus Christ's words came like a smooth, sharpened arrow, a two-edged sword.), (Noah Webster, *1828 American Dictionary of the English Language, 10th Edition*, 1998), Isaiah 49:2

A Posterity in the Earth, Genesis 45:7

A Precious Corner Stone, Isaiah 28:16

A Prince, Acts 5:31

A Prophet Mighty in Deed, Luke 24:19

A Pure River of Water of Life, Revelation 22:1

A Refiner's Fire, Malachi 3:2

A Reproach, Psalm 31:11

A Righteous Branch, Jeremiah 23:5

A River, Psalm 65:9

A Scepter, Numbers 24:17

A Seed out of Jacob, Isaiah 65:9

A Shadow from the Heat, Isaiah 4:6

A Sign, Isaiah 7:14

A Spirit, John 4:24

A Star out of Jacob, Numbers, 24:17

A Star, Malachi 4:2

A Stone, Isaiah 28:16

A Stranger, Psalm 69:8

A Strong Tower from the Enemy, Psalm 61:3

A Strong, Fenced City, Psalm 31:21

A Stumbling Stone and Rock of Offense, Romans 9:32

A Sure Foundation, Isaiah 28:16

A Tried Stone, Isaiah 28:16

Abba, Father, Mark, 14:36

Accursed of God, Deuteronomy 21:23

Advocate, 1 John 2:1

All in All, 1 Corinthians 15:28, Colossians 3:11

All Knowing, Isaiah 11:9

All My Desire, 2 Samuel 23:5

All Powerful, 1 Corinthians 6:14

Almighty, Genesis 17:1

Alpha and Omega, (The first and the last),
    Revelation 1:8, Revelation 22:13

Altogether Lovely, Solomon 5:16

Always Has Been and Always Will Be, Deuteronomy 33:27,
    Psalm 61:7, 1 Timothy 1:17, Hebrews 1:10,
    1 Peter 1:20, 23

Amen, Revelation 3:14

An Advocate at the Right Hand of the Father, 1 John 2:1

An Alien, Psalm 69:8

An Everlasting Light, Isaiah 60:19

Anchor of Hope, Hebrews 6:19

Anchor of My Soul, Hebrews 6:19

Ancient of Days, Daniel 7:9

Angel of God, Genesis 21:17, Acts 27:23

Angel of the Lord, Genesis 16:9

Anointed of the LORD or Anointed One,
Lamentations 4:20, Psalm 89:50

Anointed with the Oil of Gladness above His Fellows,
Hebrews 1:9

Anointing Oil, Exodus 35:8

Apostle, Hebrews 3:1

Apple Tree, Solomon 2:3

Arm of the Lord, Isaiah 51:9

As the Shadow of a Great Rock in a Weary Land,
Isaiah 32:2

Atonement, Romans 5:11

Author of All Life Who Is Waiting for Me, Genesis 1, Ezekiel
33:11, 1 Timothy 2:4, 2 Peter 3:9

Awesome, (Influencing with awe. The word 'terrible' translates
from Hebrew into English as 'awesome.'), (Noah Webster, *1828
American Dictionary of the English Language, 10th Edition*, 1998),
Psalm 33:8, Psalm 145:6

Babe, Luke 2:8-14

Balm of Gilead, Jeremiah 8:22

Banner of Love, Song of Solomon 2:4

Battle Axe and Weapons of War, Jeremiah 51:20

Beacon, Isaiah 30:17

Beautiful, Song of Solomon 6:4

Beautiful Savior, Psalm 48:2

Before You Is Honor and Majesty, Psalm 96:6

Beginning and Ending, Revelation 1:8

Beginning of the Creation of God, Revelation 3:14

Beloved Son, Solomon 2:16, Mark 1:11

Benevolent, Nehemiah 9:17

Bishop of My Soul, 1 Peter 2:25

Blessed and Only Potentate, 1 Timothy 6:15

Blossom of God's Love, Isaiah 35:2, John 3:16

Bountiful, (Free to give), (Noah Webster, *1828 American Dictionary of the English Language, 10th Edition*, 1998), Romans 8:32

Branch, Isaiah 4:2, Isaiah 11:1-5

Branch of Righteousness, Jeremiah 33:15

Bread from Heaven, Jeremiah 33:15

Bread of Life, John 6:32

Breaker of the Chains of Prison, Luke 8:26-35

Breath of Wisdom, Isaiah 42:5

Bridegroom, John 3:29

Bridge of Life, 1 Timothy 2:5, Romans 3:23,
    Hebrews 9:27, 2 Thessalonians 1:8-9, 1 Timothy 2:5-6,
    1 Peter 3:18, John 1:12, Revelation 3:20, John 14:14

Bright and Morning Star, Revelation 22:16

Brightness of God's Glory, Hebrews 1:3

Brightness of the Everlasting Light, Isaiah 60:19

Brother, Song of Solomon 8:1

Buckler, 2 Samuel 22:31

Builder, Hebrews 11:10

Captain of My Salvation, Hebrews 2:10

Captain of the Heavenly Hosts, Joshua 5:14

Carpenter, Mark 6:3

Carpenter's Son, Matthew 13:55

Changeless, Malachi 3:6

Changer of Hearts, John 4:4-42

Character is Changeless, Hebrews 13:8

Charter, (The instrument of a grant conferring powers, rights and privileges, from a sovereign power), (Noah Webster, *1828 American Dictionary of the English Language, 10th Edition, 1998*), 1 John 5:13, In this poem I found the word, Charter. The poem was in my Grandma's Bible,

> *This Book unfolds Jehovah's mind*
> *This Charter has been sealed with blood*
> *This Friend will all our need supply*
> *This Good Physician gives us health*
> *This Guide conducts us safe to Heaven*
> *This Letter shows us of sins forgiven*
> *This Mine affords us boundless wealth*
> *This Mountain sends forth eternal joy*
> *This Sun renewed and warming the soul*
> *This Sword both wounds and makes us whole*
> *This Voice salutes accents kind*
> *This Volume is the Word of God.*
> *-Author Unknown*

Chief Corner Stone, Ephesians 2:20

Chief Shepherd, 1 Peter 5:4

Child of the Holy Ghost, (God came as a baby, born in the

flesh.), Matthew 1:18, 23, Matthew 2:8, 11

Chosen of God, Luke 23:35

Christ a King, Luke 23:2

Christ Jesus Our Lord, Acts 15:26

Christ Jesus, John 17:3

Christ the King of Israel, Mark 9:32

Christ the Lord, Luke 2:11

Christ the Power of God, 1 Corinthians 1:24

Christ the Wisdom of God, 1 Corinthians 1:24

Christ, Son of the Blessed One, Mark 14:61

Clefts of the Rock, Song of Solomon 2:14, Isaiah 2:21

Co-Equal and Co-Eternal, Genesis 1:26, 27,
    Genesis 2:1-25, John 14:26, Acts 10:38

Comforter, John 14:26

Commander, Isaiah 55:4

Commanding King of Kings, 1 Timothy 6:15,
    Revelation 17:14

Compassionate, Psalm 78:38, Matthew 20:30-34,
    John 11:35

Confidence of All the Ends of the Earth and of Those that Are
    upon the Sea, Psalm 65:5

Conquering King, Revelation 6:2

Conqueror, Revelation 6:2

Consolation of Israel, Luke 2:25

Consuming Fire, Isaiah 30:27, 30, Isaiah 31:9, 1 Corinthians 3:13,
    Hebrews 12:29

Corner Stone, Isaiah 28:16

Counselor, Isaiah 11:2, John 14:26

Covenant Maker, Genesis 17:7

Covenant of the People, Isaiah 42:6

Covert from the Storm, Isaiah 4:6

Creator of the Ends of the Earth, Isaiah 40:28

Creator of the Heavens and the Earth, Psalm 146:6

Darling, Psalm 35:17

David, their King, Psalm 132:10-13

Day Star, 2 Peter 1:19

Dayspring from on High, Luke 1:78

Defense, Psalm 59:9

Deliverer, 2 Samuel 22:2, Psalm 18:2

Desire that None Should Perish, John 3:16, 1 Peter 3:9

Dew, Hosea 14:5

Distinct, (self existent, separate, I AM THAT I AM translates to YHVH in Hebrew, His distinct name), (Noah Webster, *1828 American Dictionary of the English Language, 10th Edition, 1998*), Exodus 3:14-15

Divine Breath that All Things Come From, Genesis 2:7

Dominating, (Predominating), (Noah Webster, *1828 American Dictionary of the English Language, 10th Edition, 1998*), Isaiah 54:17, Psalm 91:11, Psalm 103:20-21

Door of the Sheep, John 10:7

Doorway of Deliverance, John 10:9

Dwelling Place in All Generations, Psalm 90:1

Dynamic, Acts 2:27

Earnest of the Holy Spirit, Ephesians 1:14

Ebenezer, (Stone of help), *Holy Bible*, Holman Bible Publisher, Copyright 1985, Crown Reference Edition, marginal notes, 1 Samuel 7:12

Elect, Isaiah 421:1

Eliakim, (The Resurrection of God), *Cruden's Complete Concordance*, Matthew 1:13

Emmanuel, (God with us), Matthew 1:23

Enduring Dominion, Psalm 145:13

Enduring Glory, Psalm 104:31

Enduring Goodness, Psalm 23:6, Romans 8:28

Enduring Judgments, Psalm 119:160

Enduring LORD, Psalm 9:7

Enduring Love, John 3:16

Enduring Memorial, Psalm 135:13

Enduring Mercy, Jude 1:21

Enduring Praise, Psalm 111:10

Enduring Righteousness, Psalm 111:3

Enduring Substance, Hebrews 10:34

Enduring Truth, Psalm 117:2

Enduring Word, 1 Peter 1:25

Ensign of the People: to It the Gentiles Will Seek, (Ensign: any signal to assemble or to give notice.), (Noah Webster, *1828 American Dictionary of the English Language, 10th Edition*, 1998), (Gentile: pagan nations), Isaiah 11:10

Ensign on a Hill, Isaiah 30:17

Entirely Sincere, 1 Peter 2:2-3

Entrance for Me, 2 Peter 1:11

Epistle, (A writing, directed or sent, communicating intelligence to a distant person), (Noah Webster, *1828 American Dictionary of the English Language, 10th Edition,* 1998), Colossians 4:16, 1 John 5:13

Eternal Excellency, Isaiah 60:15

Eternal God in the Heavens, 2 Corinthians 5:1

Eternal King, 1 Timothy 1:17

Eternal Life, John 6:54

Eternal Life with the Father, 1 John 1:2

Eternal Power, Romans 1:20

Eternal Wisdom, Proverbs 8:23

Eternally Steadfast, (steadfast loyalty, unwavering), Lamentation 3:22, Google Dictionary

Even from Everlasting to Everlasting, You are God, (Thou art God), Psalm 90:2

Everlasting Covenant, (The Bible refers to the Everlasting Covenant that God made with the children of Israel. This covenant is in Jesus Christ.), Ezekiel 37:21, 26, Hebrews 13:20

Everlasting Father, Isaiah 9:6

Everlasting King, Jeremiah 10:10

Everlasting Light, Isaiah 60:19

Everlasting Strength, Isaiah 26:4

Everything, 1 Corinthians 15:28

Exact Image of God, (The Second Person of the Trinity is the exact image of the First Person of the Trinity.), Hebrews 1:3

Exceeding Great Reward, Genesis 15:1

Exceeding Joy, Psalm 43:4

Excellent Greatness, Psalm 148:13, Psalm 150:2

Exceptional in Your Works, Exodus 14:13-31

Expectation, Psalm 62:5

Fabulous Forgiver, (Heroic), Jeremiah 31:34

Faithful and True Each Day, Isaiah 49:7,
    1 Corinthians 1:9, John 8:26

Faithful, Isaiah 49:7, 1 Corinthians 1:9

Faithful Witness, Psalm 89:37, Revelation 1:5

Father of All, Ephesians 4:6

Father of Spirits, Hebrews 12:9

Father of the Fatherless, Psalm 68:5

Ferocious Lion, Hosea 5:14, Jeremiah 50:44

Filled with Grace That Angels Long to Understand,
    1 Peter 1:12

Finisher of Our Faith, Hebrews 12:2

First and Last, Revelation 1:11

First Begotten of the Dead, Revelation 1:5

Firstborn from the Dead, Colossians 1:18

Firstborn of Every Creature, Colossians 1:15

Firstfruits, 1 Corinthians 15:23

Firstfruits of Them that Slept, 1 Corinthians 15:20

Flower of Faith, Isaiah 40:5

For God is the King of all the Earth, Psalm 47:7

For Great is the Holy One of Israel that Is with Me,
    Isaiah 12:6

For that Thy Name Is Near Thy Wondrous Works Declare, (Your
    beautiful works in all creation show your magnificence.),
    Psalm 75:1

For the Lord God Is a Sun and Shield, Psalm 84:11

For the Lord Is a God of Knowledge and by Him Actions Are
    Weighed, 1 Samuel 2:3

For the Lord Is My Defense and the Holy One of Israel Is My King, Psalm 89:18

For the LORD Whose Name Is Jealous, Is a Jealous God, Exodus 34:14

Forceful, (Acting with power), (Noah Webster, *1828 American Dictionary of the English Language, 10th Edition*, 1998), Genesis 1:1-31

Foreordained before the Foundations of the World, 1 Peter 1:20

Forerunner, Hebrews 6:20

Forgiver of Sins, Luke 5:21-24

Forgiving, Exodus 34:7

Fortress, Psalm 18:2, Psalm 91:2, Amos 5:9

Foundation, 2 Timothy 2:19

Fountain of Life, Psalm 36:9

Fountain of Living Waters, Jeremiah 17:13

Fountain of the Water of Life, Revelation 21:6

Free Gift, Romans 5:5, 18

Friend, Song of Solomon 5:16

Friend of Sinners, Luke 7:34

Full of Compassion, Psalm 86:15

Full of Grace and Truth, John 1:14

Full of Majesty, Psalm 29:4

Full of Righteousness, Psalm 48:10

Full of Splendor, (A description of God but in this verse those words are not used. I can only imagine this.), Isaiah 6:1

Fuller's Soap, (A fuller "fulls" cloth, meaning thickens cloth, presumably with soap.), (Noah Webster, *1828 American Dictionary of the English Language, 10th Edition*, 1998), Malachi 3:2

Fullness of the Godhead, Colossian 1:19, Colossians 2:9

Gates of Righteousness, Psalm 118:19-20

Gateway of Glory, Psalm 24:9, 10

Generous, John 3:16, James 1:17

Gentle Shepherd, 2 Corinthians 2:10, Psalm 18:35

Gentle, 2 Corinthians 10:1

Gift of God, John 4:10

Giver of Eternal life, Luke 18:28-30, Titus 1:2

Glorious, Psalm 76:4, Psalm 145:12

Glorious Arm, Isaiah 63:12

Glorious Lord, Isaiah 33:21

Glory and Lifter of My Head, Psalm 3:3

Glory of God, Psalm 19:1

Glory of His Majesty, Isaiah 2:21

Glory of Israel, Joshua 7:19

God Is My Salvation, Psalm 62:7

God Is the Judge Promoting One and Demoting Another, Psalm 75:7

God Is the King of All the Earth, Psalm 47:7

God Is the Strength of My Heart, Psalm 73:26

God My Strength, Psalm 46:1

God of Abraham, Genesis 26:24

God of All the Earth, Psalm 47:7

God of Israel that Dwells between the Cherubims, Isaiah 37:16

God of Israel, Psalm 41:13

God of Jacob Is My Refuge, Psalm 46:7

God of the Ages, Hebrews 13:8

God Only Wise, Romans 16:27

God the Lord, Psalm 140:7

God with Us, Isaiah 8:8-10, Matthew 1:23

God, My Exceeding Joy, Psalm 43:4

God, the Father, Called Jesus, 'God', When He Was Manifested in the Flesh, Hebrews 1:8, 1 Timothy 3:6

God's Elect, Isaiah 65:9

God's Firstborn, Higher than the Kings of the Earth, Psalm 89:27

God's Glory, 2 Chronicles 5:13-14

God's Son, Jesus, Acts 3:26

Godhead, Colossians 2:6, 9, Romans 1:20

Golden Altar, Revelation 9:13

Good and Upright, (Goodness and Truth), Psalm 25:8

Good Shepherd, John 10:11

Good to All, Psalm 145:9

Goodness Is Limitless, Exodus 34:6

Governor among the Nations, Psalm 22:28

Governor of Governors, Matthew 2:6

Grace Angels Long to Understand, 1 Peter 1:12

Grace Is Poured into Your Lips, Psalm 45:2

Gracious Giver or Gracious Grace, (Divine Grace), (Noah Webster, 1828 American Dictionary of the English Language, 10th Edition, 1998), Nehemiah 9:17

Gracious God, Jonah 4:2

Gracious, Exodus 22:27, Psalm 145:8

Great Commander, Psalm 107:25, Amos 6:11, Luke 8:25

Great Conqueror, (of storms, Mark 6:48-51), (of demons, Mark 1:23-26), (of disease, Mark 2:1-12), (of death, Mark 5:35-42)

Great Goodness, Psalm 145:7

Great Is the Holy One of Israel, Isaiah 12:6

Great Shepherd Brought from the Dead, Hebrews 13:20

Great Shepherd of the Sheep, Hebrews 13:20

Great Worker, John 10:38, Acts 2:22

Great, Psalm 48:1-2

Greatest, Mark 9:34

Greatly Exalted, Psalm 47:9

Greatness Is Your Excellence, Exodus 15:7, Psalm 150:2

Greatness of Mercy, Nehemiah 13:22

Guide, John 16:13

Habitation of Justice, Jeremiah 31:23

Habitation, Psalm 71:3

Hammer, Jeremiah 23:29

Harbor for the Lost, Psalm 33:18, Hebrews 6:19,
    1 Peter 1:3

Has Infinite Ability, Luke 3:8, Romans 4:16-21,
    Philippians 3:21

He Came by Water and Blood, 1 John 5:6

He Has Done Excellent Things that Are Known throughout All
    the Earth, Isaiah 12:4

He has heard my voice and my cries of desperation. His ear
    listens very closely to my needs., (He is always listening for
    my prayers.), *Holy Bible*, Holman Bible Publisher, Copyright 1985,
    Crown Reference Edition, Marginal notes, Exodus 16:1-13

He Heals the Broken in Heart and Binds up Their Wounds,
    Psalm 147:3

He Is High above All People, Psalm 99:2

He is Worthy of All Praise, Psalm 70:4

He Refreshes the Soul, Proverbs 25:13

He Reigns, Revelation 19:6

He that Abides of Old, Psalm 55:19

He that Lives, Revelation 2:17

He that Ministers Seed, 2 Corinthians 9:10

He Was Begotten of the Father, John 1:14

He Will Be Our Guide Even unto Death, Psalm 48:14

He Will Never Allow the Righteous to Be Moved,
    Psalm 55:22

He Will Tread down My Enemies, Psalm 60:12

Head of Every Man, 1 Corinthians 11:3

Head of Principalities, Colossians 2:15

Head of the Church, Ephesians 5:23

Head over All Things to the Church, Ephesians 1:22

Head Stone of the Corner, Psalm 118:22

Healer of My Heart, Isaiah 61:1, Luke 4:18

Health of My Countenance, Psalm 42:11

Heaven's Glory, Luke 19:38

Heavenly Father, Matthew 6:14

Heir of All Things, Hebrews 1:2

Helper of the Fatherless, Psalm 10:14

Hidden Manna, Revelation 2:17

Hiding Place, Psalm 32:7

Hiding Place from the Wind, Isaiah 32:2

High Is Your Right Hand, Psalm 89:13

High Priest, Genesis 14:18, Hebrews 8:1

High, Psalm 21:7

Highest, Psalm 18:13

Highway, Isaiah 35:8

His Excellency, Psalm 62:4

His Greatness Is Unsearchable, Psalm 145:3

His Name Alone Is Excellent, Psalm 148:13

His Name Is Exalted, Isaiah 12:4

His Understanding is Infinite, Psalm 147:5

Holiness of God, Psalm 29:2, 8; Psalm 47:8, Psalm 110:3

Holiness, (Characteristic of Jesus Christ), Psalm 108:7

Hollow of God's Hand, Isaiah 40:12

Holy Arm, Isaiah 52:10

Holy Child Jesus, Acts 4:27

Holy Child of Bethlehem, Matthew 2:8

Holy Ghost, 1 John 5:7

Holy in All Your Works, Psalm 145:17

Holy One of God, Mark 1:24

Holy One of Israel, 2 Kings 19:22

Holy Servant, (The first verse referenced has the words in it separately, Holy and Servant. Jesus was the holiest example of a servant of God.), Isaiah 49:7, Matthew 12:18

Holy Spirit Refreshment, (New Life, Fresh Strength, A benefit that God gives to us who are in Christ), (Noah Webster, *1828 American Dictionary of the English Language*, *10th Edition*, 1998), Proverbs 12:28

Holy Spirit, Psalm 51:11

Holy Thing, Luke 1:35

Holy, Harmless, and Undefiled, Hebrews 7:26

Holy, Psalm 99:5, Psalm 111:9

Hope, Joel 3:16

Hope Forever, Titus 1:2

Hope of Earth, Luke 15:7

Horn of Salvation, Luke 1:69

House of Defense, Psalm 31:2

Husband, Isaiah 54:5

I AM THAT I AM, Exodus 3:14

I AM, Exodus 3:14, John 8:58

Image of the Invisible God, Colossians 1:15

Immanuel, (God with us incarnate in Jesus Christ. God is not a distant God. He is a God who is close to us because He lived a human life!), (Eric Celerier's email sent in August 2019), Isaiah 8:8, Matthew 1:23

Immovable, Proverbs 10:25

Immutable, Hebrews 6:13-19

Impartial, Matthew 5:45, John 4:14, Revelation 22:12

In Him I Live and Move and Have My Being, Acts 17:28

In the Beginning You Made the Foundation of the Earth and the Heavens Are the Works of Your Hands, Hebrews 1:10

In You Is Life and Your Life Was the Light of Man, John 1:4

In Your Presence there Is no Darkness, Colossians 1:12-14, 1 John 1:5

Incorruptible, 1 Peter 1:23

Incorruptible Inheritance, 1 Peter 1:4

Incredible, (Unbelievable), Ephesians 3:20

Indescribable, 2 Corinthians 12:4, Revelation 4:3-11

Infallible, (Not fallible, not capable of erring), (Noah Webster, *1828 American Dictionary of the English Language, 10th Edition*, 1998), Acts 1:3

Infinite, Psalm 147:5, 1 Timothy 1:17

Infinite Understanding, Psalm 147:5

Inseparable Love for Me, Romans 8:39

Inspiring, Job 32:8, 2 Timothy 3:16

Intercessor, Isaiah 59:16

Invincible, (This word is not found in the verse but the idea is there.), Ephesians 1:19-20

Invisible, 1 Timothy 1:17, Hebrews 11:27

Irresistible, Isaiah 14:27, Revelation 6:174

Jealous, Exodus 20:5

Jealous God, Exodus 34:14

Jehovah, Psalm 83:18

Jesus, Matthew 1:21

Jesus and the Father are one, John 10:30, John 17:11

Jesus Christ of the Seed of David, 2 Timothy 2:8

Jesus Christ, Matthew 1:1

Jesus Christ, My Savior, Philippians 3:20, 1 Timothy 1:1

Jesus Christ, the Oracle of God, Deuteronomy 18:18

Jesus Christ, the Righteous, 1 John 2:1

Jesus of Nazareth, a Man Approved of God among Us by Miracles and Wonders and Signs, which God Did by Him in the Midst of Mankind, Acts 2:23

Jesus the Prophet of Nazareth of Galilee, Matthew 21:11

Jesus, the Lamb of God, John 1:36

Jewel of Glory, Revelation 4:3-11

Jewel of Heaven, Revelation 4:3-11

Joy Giver, Psalm 16:11

Joy of Heaven, 1 Corinthians 3:7

Judge, Psalm 50:6, Romans 2:6

Judge of the Earth, Psalm 94:2

Judge of the Fatherless and the Oppressed, Psalm 10:18

Judge of the Quick and the Dead, (Quick: alive, living; opposed to dead or unanimated), (Noah Webster, *1828 American Dictionary of the English Language, 10th Edition, 1998)*, Acts 10:42

Judge of the Widows, Psalm 68:5

Just, Deuteronomy 32:4, Proverbs 16:11, Romans 2:2-16

Just and True Are Your Ways, Revelation 15:3

Just One, Acts 7:52

Keeper of My Soul, Psalm 121:5

Keeper of the Covenant, Deuteronomy 7:12, Daniel 9:4

Keeper of the Vineyard, John 15:1

Key of David, Revelation 3:7

Key of Knowledge, Luke 11:52

Kind, 1 Corinthians 13:4

King Forever, Psalm 29:10

King of Creation, John 1:1-3

King of Glory, Psalm 24:7

King of Heaven, Luke 19:38

King of Kings, Daniel 2:37, Revelation 17:14

King of Nations, Jeremiah 10:7

King of Peace, Hebrews 7:2

King of Righteousness, Isaiah 32:1

King of Saints, Revelation 15:3

King of Salem, Hebrews 7:1

King of the Ages, 1 Timothy 1:17

King of the Daughter of Zion, Jeremiah 8:19,
    Zechariah 9:9

King of the Jews, Mark 15:2

Knowledge, Proverbs 2:5, 10

Lamb of God that Takes Away the Sins of the World,
    John 1:29

Lamb of God that Was Slain, Revelation 5:6

Lamb, 1 Peter 1:19, Revelation 17:14

Last Adam, 1 Corinthians 15:45

Law of the Lord, Psalm 1:2

Lawgiver, James 4:12

Lenient, Romans 2:4, Romans 8:32

Let God Be Magnified, Psalm 70:4

Letter (A written or printed message, an epistle), (Noah Webster,
    1828 American Dictionary of the English Language, 10th Edition, 1998),
    1 John 5:13

Light of Israel, Isaiah 10:17

Light of the World, Matthew 5:14, John 8:12, John 11:9

Light, Genesis 1:1-3, 1 John 1:5

Lighthouse, (Beacon on the Mountain), Isaiah 30:17

Lily of the Valleys, Solomon 2:1

Lion of the House of Judah, Hosea 5:14

Lion of the Tribe of Judah, (spelling in the King James Version,
    'Juda'), Revelation 5:5

Light of Life, John 8:12

Lively Hope, (Living Hope), 1 Peter 1:3

Living Bread, John 6:51

Living God, Psalm 115:3-8, Jeremiah 10:10, John 6:69

Living Way, Hebrews 10:20

Living Word, John 1:1, 14

Long Awaited Precious Promise, Hebrew 9:15

Lord of All, Acts 10:36

Lord of Glory, 1 Corinthians 2:8

Lord of Hosts, Psalm 46:7

Lord of Lords, Deuteronomy 10:17, Psalm 136:3,
    Revelation 17:14

Lord of the Sabbath, Mark 2:28, Luke 6:5

Love, 1 John 4:8

Love Is Limitless, Ephesians 1:6, Jude 1:21

Lovely, Song of Solomon 5:16, Philippians 4:8

Loves His Blood-Washed Church, Acts 20:28,
    Ephesians 1:3-14

Lovingkindness, Psalm 103:4

Lowly, (Not Lofty, When He came to earth He came humbly),
    (Noah Webster, *1828 American Dictionary of the English Language, 10th
    Edition*, 1998), Zechariah 9:9

Magnificent, Psalm 72:19, Psalm 145:5

Magnified, Psalm 70:4

Majestic, (He is clothed with majesty.), Psalm 93:1

Man of Sorrows, Isaiah 53:3

Man of War, Exodus 15:3

Manifested in the Flesh, Matthew 1:22, 23, John 1:1, 14

Manifold Wisdom, Ephesians 3:10

Marvelous Are Your Works, Psalm 104:24, Psalm 92:5

Marvelous Light, Isaiah 60:1

Master, Matthew 8:19

Mediator of a Better Covenant, Hebrews 8:6

Meek, 2 Corinthians 10:1

Melchizedek, (The Father called Jesus a High Priest, saying, You
are a priest for ever after the order of Melchizedek, Psalm
110:4, Hebrews 6:20). (Melchizedek interpreted is the King of
Righteousness, Hebrews 7:2), (Jesus is an High Priest of the
order of Melchizedek, set on the right hand of the throne of
Majesty in Heaven, Romans 8:1)

Merciful,

- Psalm 62:12 "Also unto thee, O LORD, belongeth mercy."
- Psalm 37:26 "He is ever merciful, and lendeth"
- Psalm 103:12 "As far as the east is from the west, so far hath
  he removed our transgressions from us."
- Psalm 136:1-26 "O give thanks unto the LORD; for he is
  good: for his mercy endureth forever. O give thanks to the
  God of gods: for his mercy endureth forever. O give thanks
  to the LORD of lords: for his mercy endureth forever. To
  him who alone doeth great wonders: for his mercy endureth
  for ever. To him that by wisdom made the heavens: for his
  mercy endureth for ever. To him that stretched out the
  earth above the waters: for his mercy endureth for ever. To
  him that made great lights: for his mercy endureth for ever:
  The sun to rule by day: for his mercy endureth for ever: The
  moon and stars to rule by night: for his mercy endureth for
  ever. To him that smote Egypt in their first-born: for his
  mercy endureth forever: And brought out Israel from
  among them: for his mercy endureth for ever: With a strong
  hand, and with a stretched-out arm: for his mercy endureth
  for ever. To him which divided the Red sea into parts: for
  his mercy endureth forever: And made Israel to pass
  through the midst of it: for his mercy endureth forever: But

overthrew Pharaoh and his host in the Red sea: for his mercy endureth forever. To him which led his people through the wilderness: for his mercy endureth forever. To him which smote great kings: for his mercy endureth for ever: And slew famous kings: for his mercy endureth for ever: Sihon king of the Amorites: for his mercy endureth for ever: And Og the king of Bashan: for his mercy endureth for ever: And gave their land for an heritage: for his mercy endureth for ever: Even an heritage unto Israel his servant: for his mercy endureth for ever. Who remembered us in our low estate: for his mercy endureth for ever. And hath redeemed us from our enemies: for his mercy endureth forever. Who giveth food to all flesh: for his mercy endureth for ever. O give thanks unto the God of heaven: for his mercy endureth for ever."

- Matthew 9:36 "But when he saw the multitudes, he was moved with compassion on them, because they fainted, and were scattered abroad, a sheep having no shepherd."

- Matthew 9:18, 25 "While he spake these things unto them, behold, there came a certain ruler, and worshipped him, saying, My daughter is even now dead: but come and lay thy hand upon her, and she shall live. ... But when the people were put forth, he went in, and took her by the hand, and the maid arose."

- Luke 23:34 "Then said Jesus, Father, forgive them: for they know not what they do."

- John 3:16-17 "For God so loved the world, that he gave his only begotten Son, that whosoever believeth in him should not perish, but have everlasting life. For God sent not his Son into the world to condemn the world, but that the world through him might be saved."

- 1 Peter 1:3 "Blessed be the God and Father of our Lord Jesus Christ, which according to his abundant mercy hath begotten us again unto a lively hope by the resurrection of Jesus Christ from the dead."

Messiah, John 4:25

Messiah the Prince, Daniel 9:25

Mighty, Psalm 24:8

Mighty Arm, Job 35:9

Mighty God, Isaiah 9:6

Mighty to Save, Isaiah 63:1

Mine, (When I followed in obedience what Romans 10:13 said, then Jesus became mine.), Solomon 2:16

Minister of Circumcision, Colossian 2:11

Minister of the Sanctuary, Hebrews 8:2

Minister of the Tabernacle, Hebrews 8:2

Mirror, (Reference to 'glass 'and 'same image from glory to glory 'reminds me of the reflection from a mirror.), 2 Corinthians 3:18

Mirror of God's Word, 2 Corinthians 3:18

Morning Star, Revelation 2:28

Most High for Evermore, Psalm 92:8

Most High over All the Earth, Psalm 82:18

Most Upright, Isaiah 26:7

Mountain of Holiness, Jeremiah 31:23

Mountain, Psalm 78:54

Multifaceted, (Having many facets, or aspects), (Noah Webster, *1828 American Dictionary of the English Language, 10th Edition*, 1998), Ephesians 3:10

My Bread, Proverbs 9:5

My Chief Joy, Psalm 137:6

My Drink, Proverbs 9:5

My Fortress, Psalm 144:2

My Glory, Psalm 62:7

My God, Psalm 3:7

My God Is the Rock of My Refuge, Psalm 94:22

My God, My Glory, Isaiah 60:19

My Goodness, Psalm 144:2

My Helper, Psalm 54:4, 2 Timothy 4:18

My Holy Mountain, Isaiah 65:11

My Hope, Jeremiah 17:17

My Inspiration, Job 32:8

My King, Psalm 2:6

My Meat, John 4:32

My Portion Forever, Psalm 73:26

My Redeemer Is Strong; the LORD of Hosts Is His Name,
    Jeremiah 51:34

My Redeemer, Isaiah 41:14

My Restorer, Isaiah 58:12

My Righteousness, Malachi 4:2, Jeremiah 23:6

My Savior, Isaiah 60:16

My Shield, He in whom I Trust, Psalm 144:2

My Stay, (Continuance in a place, abode for a indefinite time),
    (Noah Webster, *1828 American Dictionary of the English Language, 10th
    Edition,* 1998), 2 Samuel 22:19, Psalm 18:18

My Strength, Psalm 81:1

My Tabernacle, Psalm 61:4

Nazarene, Matthew 2:23

Never Changes, Hebrews 13:8, James 1:17

No Respecter of Persons, 1 Peter 1:17

Nothing I Desire Compares with You, Psalm 97:2

O God My Savior, Isaiah 45:15

O God of Jacob, Psalm 76:6

O God of My Righteousness, Psalm 4:1

O God of My Salvation, Psalm 27:9

O God, My God, Psalm 43:4

O God, My Shield, Psalm 84:9

O Lord God of Truth, Psalm 31:5

O Lord of Hosts, Psalm 84:12

O Lord, My God, My Holy One, Habakkuk 1:12

O the Hope of Israel, the Savior, Jeremiah 14:8

O, Most Mighty, Psalm 45:3

O, Thou (You, God) that Dwells in the Heavens,
    Psalm 123:1

O, Thou (You, God) that Inhabits the Praise of Israel, Psalm 22:3

Obedient to the Father, Luke 22:42

Of Great Kindness, Jonah 4:2

Of Great Mercy, Psalm 145:8

Of Great Power, Psalm 147:5

Office Is Manifold (Of diverse kinds, many in time, appearing at
    diverse times, or in various ways), (Noah Webster, *1828 American
    Dictionary of the English Language, 10th Edition*, 1998),
    Ephesians 3:10, 1 Peter 4:10

Offspring of David, Revelation 22:16

Omnipotent, Revelation 19:6

Omnipresent, Exodus 3:14, Proverbs 15:3, Proverbs 24:12

Omniscient, 1 John 3:20

One Chosen Out of Your People, Psalm 89:19

One that Is Mighty, Psalm 89:19

One with the Father, John 1:1

Only Begotten, John 1:14

Only One Able, Genesis 1:1, James 4:12

Open Door, Revelation 3:8
Our Captain, Hebrews 2:10
Our Father, Isaiah 63:16
Our Maker, Psalm 95:6
Our Safe Haven, (Our Desired Haven), Psalm 107:30
Paraclete, (Comforter), John 14:16
Pathway of Righteousness, Proverbs 12:28
Patient, Romans 2:7
Peace, Ephesians 2:14
Perfector of My Faith, Psalm 138:8
Perfect Light, Proverbs 4:8, Isaiah 60:1, 2 Peter 1:1
Perfect Love, 1 John 4:18
Perfect Sacrifice, Hebrews 9:26
Perfection of Beauty, Psalm 50:2
Pitiful, James 5:11
Porter, John 10:3
Portion of My Cup, Psalm 16:5

Portion of My Inheritance, (Security from failure or decline, support, protection, defense), Psalm 16:5

Power is Limitless

- Psalm 62:11 "Power belongeth unto God, …"
- Romans 8:11 "But if the Spirit of him that raised up Jesus from the dead dwell in you, he that raised up Christ from the dead shall also quicken your mortal bodies by his Spirit that dwelleth in you."
- Ephesians 1:19, 20 "And what is the exceeding greatness of his power to usward who believe, according to the working of his mighty power,
  Which he wrought in Christ, when he raised him from the dead, and set him at his own right hand in the heavenly places,"
- John 10:17, 18 "Therefore doth my Father love me, because I lay down my life, that I might take it again. No man taketh it from me, but I lay it down of myself. I have power to lay it down, and I have power to take it again. This commandment have I received of my Father."
- 1 Corinthians 6:14 "And God hath both raised up the Lord, and will also raise up us by his own power."
- 2 Corinthians 4:14 "Knowing, that he which raised up the Lord Jesus, shall raise up us also by Jesus, and shall present us with you."

Precious, 1 Peter 1:2-7, 1 Peter 2:7

Preeminent, Colossians 1:16-18

Presents Us Faultless before the Presence of His Glory with Great Joy, Jude 24

Priest, Hebrews 7:20-22

Prince of Glory, Psalm 8:1, Psalm 24:10

Prince of Life, Acts 3:15

Prince of Peace, Isaiah 9:6

Prince of the Kings of the Earth, Joel 3:16, Revelation 1:5

Prisoners Set Free, Luke 8:26-35

Prophet, Hosea 12:13

Propitiation, (sacrifice), Romans 3:25, 1 John 2:2

Protector, Psalm 23

Providential, (Proceeding from divine direction or superintendence), (Noah Webster, *1828 American Dictionary of the English Language, 10th Edition*, 1998), Lamentations 3:18-21, 24

Provider, Genesis 22:8, 14

Punisher of Evil Doers, Romans 2:8, 9

Purification, 2 Chronicles 30:19

Quickening Spirit, 1 Corinthians 15:45-47

Quiet Rest, Matthew 11:28

Rabbi, John 1:38

Rabboni, (Master), John 20:16

Rain and Showers, Deuteronomy 32:2

Raised from the Dead, Acts 3:15, Romans 6:9, 1 Peter 1:19-21

Ransom for All, 1 Timothy 2:6

Reconciliation, Daniel 9:24

Refiner and Purifier of Silver, Malachi 3:3

Refiner's Fire, Malachi 3:2

Refuge for My Soul, Psalm 57:1

Refuge, Psalm 91:2

Repairer of the Breach, Isaiah 58:12

Resting Place, Jeremiah 50:6

Restorer of the Paths, Isaiah 58:12

Resurrection and the Life, John 11:25

Revealer of Secrets, Daniel 2:28

Reverend, Psalm 111:9

Righteous, Psalm 92:15, Isaiah 42:21, Exodus 9:27

Righteous Branch, Jeremiah 23:5

Righteous in All Your Ways, Psalm 145:7

Righteous Judge, 2 Timothy 4:8

Righteous Man, Isaiah 41:2

Righteous One, Romans 5:19

Righteousness of the Perfect, Proverbs 11:5

Risen Christ, Romans 8:34

Rivers of My Pleasure, Psalm 36:8

Rivers of Living Water, John 7:38

Rivers of Water in a Dry Place, Isaiah 32:2

Roadway of Righteousness, 1 Corinthians 1:30, John 14:6

Rock, Psalm 92:15

Rock of Ages, Psalm 25:6, Psalm 40:2, Psalm 78:35

Rock of Habitation, Psalm 71:3

Rock of Israel, 2 Samuel 23:3

Rock of My Heart, Psalm 61:2, Psalm 72:19

Rock of My Refuge, Psalm 94:22

Rock of My Strength, Psalm 62:7

Rock of Offence, Isaiah 8:14

Rock of Our Salvation, Psalm 95:1

Rod of Iron, Revelation 12:5

Rod of Jesse, Isaiah 11:1

Root of David, Revelation 5:5

Root of Jesse, Isaiah 11:10

Rose of Bethlehem, Isaiah 35:1

Rose of Sharon, Song of Solomon 2:1

Royal Master, Matthew 22:36, Matthew 23:10,
Colossians 4:1

Ruler in Israel, Micah 5:2

Ruler of the Nations, Psalm 72:11

Sacrifice, 1 Peter 1:18, 19

Sacrificial Lamb, 1 Peter 1:18-19

Salvation of God, Luke 3:6

Salvation of Israel, Psalm 14:7

Salvation, Psalm 118:14

Sanctification, 1 Corinthians 1:30

Sanctifier, Genesis 2:2, Psalm 8:4, Philippians 1:16, 2:13;
Acts 17:28

Sanctuary, Hebrews 9:2

Saves, Regenerates, and Renews, Titus 3:5

Saving Strength of His Right Hand, Psalm 20:6

Savior, Luke 1:47

Scalpel, (small, light, usually straight knife used in surgical and anatomical operations), (Random House Reference, *The Random House Webster's College Dictionary, [The Unabridged Edition],* 1999), Ezekiel 11:19, Ezekiel 36:26

Scepter of Righteousness, Hebrews 1:8

Secret Place, Psalm 91:1

Secret Places of the Stairs, Song of Solomon 2:14

Security, Matthew 28:14

Seed of the Woman, Genesis 3:15

Self-Existent that Always Has Been, Exodus 3:14-15

Selfless, Matthew 20:28

Serious, Nahum 1:2-7

Servant of Rulers, Isaiah 49:7

Servant, Matthew 12:18

Sharp Sword, Revelation 2:12

Shelter in Rain, Isaiah 4:6

Shelter in Time of Storm, Psalm 61:3

Shelter, Psalm 61:3

Shepherd of Israel, Psalm 80:1

Shepherd of My Soul, Psalm 51:12, Psalm 100:3

Shepherd of the Flock, Isaiah 63:11

Shepherd of the Sheep, Psalm 23, John 10:2, 11

Shepherd through Pain, Psalm 23:1

Shield, Psalm 91:4

Shiloh, Genesis 49:10

Sinless, John 7:18, 1 Peter 1:19

Slayer of Sins, Romans 6:9-11

Slow to Anger, Psalm 103:8

Son of Abraham, Luke 3:34

Son of David, Matthew 1:1

Son of God, Matthew 4:3, Luke 1:35

Son of Jacob, Luke 3:34

Son of Man, Mark 2:10

Son of Mary, Matthew 1:21, Mark 6:3

Son of the Blessed, Mark 14:61

Son of the Father, John 1:18

Son of the Highest, Luke 1:32

Son of the Most High, Mark 5:7

Song, Exodus 15:2

Sovereign, (Supreme Power) Noah Webster, *1828 Dictionary of the English Language*, Genesis 17:1, Genesis 14:18-20,

Spirit of Burning, Isaiah 4:4

Spirit of Christ, 1 Peter 1:11

Spirit of Glory, 1 Peter 4:14

Spirit of God, 1 Corinthians 3:16

Spirit of Grace, Hebrews 10:29

Spirit of His Son, Galatians 4:6

Spirit of Jesus Christ, Philippians 1:19

Spirit of Life, Romans 8:2

Spirit of Promise, Ephesians 1:13

Spirit of the Living God, 2 Corinthians 3:3

Spirit of the Lord God, Isaiah 61:1

Spirit of the Lord, Isaiah 11:2

Spirit of Truth, John 14:17

Spiritual Drink, 1 Corinthians 10:4

Spiritual Meat, 1 Corinthians 10:3

Spiritual Rock, 1 Corinthians 10:4

Splendorous, (Great Brightness), (Noah Webster, *1828 American Dictionary of the English Language, 10th Edition*, 1998), Daniel 7:9

Star of Love, 2 Peter 1:19, Revelation 2:28

Star out of Israel, Numbers 24:17

Star out of Jacob, Numbers 24:17

Steadfast, Hebrews 13:8, Daniel 6:26

Stone of Stumbling, Isaiah 8:14

Strength in Time of Trouble, Psalm 37:39

Strength of the Children of Israel, Joel 3:16

Strength, Psalm 118:14

Strong, (Characteristic of God), Isaiah 28:2

Strong City, Psalm 60:9

Strong Habitation, Psalm 71:3

Strong is Your Hand, Psalm 89:13

Strong One Who Keeps Covenants, (By His righteousness we have our righteousness.), Jeremiah 23:6

Strong One, Isaiah 28:2

Strong Rock, Psalm 31:2

Strong Tower from the Enemy, Psalm 61:3

Strongest, Isaiah 13:6, Ezekiel 10:5

Substitute, 1 Peter 1:18, 19

Sufficient One, 2 Corinthians 12:9

Sun, Psalm 84:11

Sun of Righteousness, Malachi 4:2

Superior, (Greater in excellence; surpassing others in greatness), (Noah Webster, *1828 American Dictionary of the English Language, 10th Edition*, 1998), Isaiah 28:29,

1 John 4:18, 19

Supreme Sacrifice for My Sins, Ephesians 5:2

Supreme, (Glorified to the highest degree),
Ephesians 1:6, 21, Ephesians 3:20, Ephesians 4:10

Sure, Hebrews 6:19

Surety, (Certainty, unquestionable(Noah Webster, *1828 American
Dictionary of the English Language, 10th Edition, 1998*), Hebrews 7:22

Sustainer, Psalm 55:22

Sword, Isaiah 66:16

Teacher that Came from God, John 3:2

Tender Mercies, Psalm 25:6

Terrible, (Adapted to impress dread, terror or solemn awe,
[characteristic of God]), (Noah Webster, *1828 American Dictionary
of the English Language, 10th Edition, 1998*), Psalm 47:2, Psalm 99:3

That Holy Spirit of Promise which Is the Earnest of My
Inheritance until the Redemption of the Purchased
Possession, unto the Praise of His Glory,
Ephesians 1:13, 14

The Air I Breathe, Isaiah 42:5, Acts 17:25

The Almighty, Genesis 49:25

The Amen, the Faithful and True Witness, the Beginning of the Creation of God, Revelation 3:14

The Beginning of the Creation of God, Revelation 3:14

The Brightness of His Glory and the Express Image of His Person, Hebrews 1:2

The Christ, Matthew 26:63

The Christ, the Savior of the World, John 4:42

The Confidence I Have, Hebrews 7:22

The Confidence of All the Ends of the Earth, Psalm 65:5

The Covert of God's Wings, Psalm 61:4

The Darling from Heaven, Psalm 22:20, Psalm 35:17

The Eternal God in the Heavens, 2 Corinthians 5:1

The Eternal Life with the Father, 1 John 1:2

The Everlasting Father, Isaiah 9:6

The Everlasting God, Genesis 21:33

The Exalted One, Chosen out of the People, Psalm 89:19

The Excellency of Jacob Whom God Loved, Psalm 47:4

The Father, Husbandman, John 15:1

The God of all Flesh, Jeremiah 32:27

The God of Eternity, Isaiah 57:15, 1 John 1:2

The God of Israel Is He that Gives Strength and Power unto His People, Psalm 68:35

The God of My Life, Psalm 42:8

The God of My Strength, Psalm 43:2

The Goodness of God that Endures Continually, Psalm 52:1

The Government Will Be upon His Shoulder, Isaiah 9:6

The Great I Am, Exodus 15:3

The Great Physician, Exodus 15:26, Matthew 4:23

The Great, the Mighty God, the LORD of Hosts, Great in Counsel, Mighty in Your Works, Jeremiah 32:18, 19

The Head over All Things to the Church, Ephesians 1:22

The Head Stone of the Corner, Psalm 118:22

The Help of My Countenance, Psalm 42:5

The High and Lofty One that Inhabits Eternity, Isaiah 57:15

The Highest among Ten Thousands, (The Chiefest among Ten Thousands), Song of Solomon 5:10

The Highest, Psalm 18:13, Luke 1:32

The Holy One of Israel Is My King, Psalm 89:18

The Holy One of Israel, Psalm 78:41

The Hope I Carry, (My Hope), 1 Timothy 1:1

The Hope of Israel, Jeremiah 14:8, Acts 28:20

The Hope of Our Fathers, Jeremiah 50:7

The Horn of His People, Psalm 148:14

The Interpreter, Genesis 40:8

The King of Israel, John 1:49

The Lamb in the Midst of the Church, Revelation 5:6-10

The Lamb of God which Takes Away the Sin of the World, John 1:29

The Life, John 14:6

The Light of Men, John 1:4, 14

The Light of the Morning, Isaiah 58:8

The Light of the World, John 9:5

The Light that Shines Unto the Perfect Day, Proverbs 4:18

The LORD Executes Righteousness and Judgment for All that Are Oppressed, Psalm 103:6

The Lord God of Israel Who only Does Wondrous Things, Psalm 72:18

The Lord Is a Man of War, Exodus 15:3

The LORD Is Good to All and His Tender Mercies Are over All His Works, Psalm 145:9

The LORD Is My Portion of My Inheritance, Psalm 16:5

The LORD Is on My Side, Psalm 118:6

The LORD Is the Refuge of the Poor, Psalm 14:6

The Lord Lets the Prisoner Go Free, (The Lord Looseth the Prisoners), Psalm 146:8

The Lord of Hosts; the Whole Earth Is Full of Your Glory, Isaiah 6:3

The Lord of the Whole Earth, Psalm 97:5

The LORD Opens the Eyes of the Blind, Psalm 146:8

The LORD Our Righteousness, Jeremiah 23:6

The LORD Preserves the Faithful and Fully Rewards the Proud Person, Psalm 31:23

The LORD Preserves the Simple or the LORD Keeps the Humble, Psalm 116:6

The LORD Reigns, Psalm 93:1

The LORD Strong and Mighty, the LORD, Mighty in Battle, Psalm 24:8

The Lord that Heals Me, (The Lord that Heals Thee), Exodus 15:26

The Lord that Lifts Up the Meek and Casts the Wicked to the Ground, Psalm 147:6

The LORD which Dwells in Zion, Psalm 9:11

The LORD Will Be A Refuge for the Oppressed, A Refuge in Times of Trouble, Psalm 9:9

The Lord, My Miracle, Mark 6:52, John 6:14

The Lord, the King, Psalm 98:6

The LORD, the Maker, Jeremiah 33:2

The Lord, the Righteous Judge, 2 Timothy 4:8

The Love of My Life, Mark 12:30

The Mercy Seat, Exodus 25:21-22

The Mighty God of Jacob, Genesis 49:24, Psalm 132:2

The Mighty One of Jacob, Isaiah 60:16

The Most High God, Psalm 57:2

The Most High God, the Possessor of the Heaven and Earth, Genesis 14:19

The Name above All Names Given among Men that We Might Be Saved, Philippians 2:9, Acts 4:12

The Offering, Hebrews 10:10

The Oil of Gladness, Psalm 45:7

The One for Whom Long Centuries Have Waited, the Messiah, John 4:25

The Only Living God, Isaiah 43:10, Isaiah 45:18

The Passover Lamb, Exodus 12:21, Exodus 12:5, 1 Peter 1:19

The Perfection of Beauty, Psalm 50:2

The Praise of All the Saints, Psalm 148:14

The Prince of Peace, Isaiah 9:6

The Prince of the Kings of the Earth, Revelation 1:5

The Redeemer, Psalm 19:14, Psalm 78:35

The Resurrection, John 11:25-27

The Right Hand of the Lord Does Valiantly, Psalm 118:15

The Right Hand of the LORD Is Exalted, Psalm 118:16

The Righteous God Tries the Hearts and Reins, Psalm 7:9

The Righteous, Psalm 141:5

Day 11

The Rock is Christ, 1 Corinthians 10:4

The Rock that Is Higher Than I, Psalm 61:2

The Rod of God's Strength out of Zion, Psalm 110:2

The Root of David, Revelation 5:5

The Salvation the Prophets Asked about and Searched for,
   1 Peter 1:10

The Sanctuary, Exodus 15:17

The Saving Strength of His Right Hand, Psalm 20:6

The Savior in Time of Trouble, Jeremiah 14:8

The Secret Place of His Tabernacle, Psalm 27:5

The Secret Places of Thunder, Psalm 81:7

The Sent of the Father, (My Father Hath Sent Me),
   John 20:21

The Shepherd, the Stone of Israel, Genesis 49:24

The Sign of the Prophet Jonas, Matthew 12:39

The Son of Man in Heaven, Revelation 1:13-16

The Son of Man whom You Have Made Strong for Yourself,
   Psalm 80:17

The Staff, Psalm 23:4

The Still Existing One that Reveals Himself, (I AM), Exodus 3:14

The Stone which the Builders Refused Is Become the Head
   Stone of the Corner, Psalm 118:22

The Stone which the Builders Rejected Has Become the Head of
   the Corner, Matthew 21:42

The Strength of My Salvation, Psalm 140:7

The Sword of the Lord, Isaiah 34:6

The Temple, Matthew 23:16

The Trier of My Heart, Psalm 17:3

The True God, Jeremiah 10:10

The True Light, 1 John 1:9

The Truth, John 14:6

The Very Word of God Incarnate, Matthew 1:20-21,
John 1:1, 14

The Voice of the Lord Is Powerful, Psalm 29:4

The Way of Holiness, Isaiah 35:8

The Way, John 14:6

The Wine God Has Mingled, Proverbs 9:5

The Word of God, Isaiah 40:8

The Word Was God, John 1:1

The Word Was Made Flesh, John 1:14

The Works of His Hand Are Truth and Judgment: All His
Commandments Are Forever, Psalm 111:7

The Worm, Job 25:6

There Is No Other God So Great as Our God,
Psalm 77:13

These Three Are One, 1 John 5:5-7

This Glorious and Fearful Name, the LORD My God,
Deuteronomy 28:58

This Is Jesus Christ, Acts 17:3

Through the Greatness of Your Power Your Enemies Will Submit
to You, Psalm 66:3

Timeless, John 8:5, Hebrews 13:8

Transport, Ephesians 2, Colossians 1:13

Treasure in Earthen Vessels, 2 Corinthians 4:7

Tree of Life, Revelation 22:14

Tried Stone, Isaiah 28:16

Triune God, John 14:26, Acts 10:38, 1 John 5:7

True, Psalm 111:7, John 8:26

True Bread, John 6:32

True God, John 17:3

True Light, 1 John 2:8

True One, John 17:3

True Vine, John 15:1

Truth, Psalm 85:11, John 14:6

Unchangeable Priesthood, Hebrews 7:24

Unchanging, Malachi 3:6

Undefiled, Song of Solomon 6:9

Understanding, Isaiah 11:2

Unfailing, Hebrews 13:5

Unquestionable, Revelation 3:14

Unquestionable, Unlimited Love, Romans 8:35-39,
    John 3:16, Hebrews 13:5

Unsearchable Greatness, Psalm 145:3

Unsearchable Judgments, Romans 11:33

Unsearchable Riches, Ephesians 3:8

Unspeakable Joy, 1 Peter 1:8

Unspeakably Rich, Psalm 24:1

Unstoppable, Romans 8:39

Unswervingly Loyal, Lamentations 3:22

Upholds All Things by the Word of His Power,
    Hebrews 1:3

Upright, (Honest, not deviating from correct moral principles),
    (Noah Webster, *1828 American Dictionary of the English Language, 10th
    Edition*, 1998), Psalm 92:15,

Valiant, Song of Solomon 3:7

Vengeful against Disobedience, 2 Thessalonians 1:8

Very Great, Ephesians 1:19-22, 1 Timothy 1:17,

Revelation 11:15-17

Victorious

- Isaiah 25:8 "He will swallow up death in victory; and the Lord God will wipe away tears from off all faces; and the rebuke of his people shall he take away from off all the earth: for the Lord hath spoken it."
- Isaiah 54:17 "No weapon that is formed against thee shall prosper;"
- Acts 3:15 "And killed the Prince of life, whom God hath raised from the dead;"
- Ephesians1:19-22 "And what is the exceeding greatness of his power to us-ward who believe, according to the working of his mighty power, Which he wrought in Christ, when he raised him from the dead, and set him at his own right hand in the heavenly places, Far above all principality, and power, and might, and dominion, and every name that is named, not only in this world, but also in that which is to come: And hath put all things under his feet, and gave him to be the head over all things to the church,"

Victorious Warrior, Exodus 15:3, Isaiah 25:8, Ephesians 2:19-22

Vine, John 15:1

Virgin Born, Isaiah 7:14, Matthew 1:23

Volume (The Scriptures or sacred writings, in a single volume, are called the *Bible*), (Noah Webster, *1828 American Dictionary of the English Language, 10th Edition*, 1998), Psalm 40:7, Hebrews 10:7

Volume of the Book, Psalm 40:7

Wall of Fire, Zechariah 2:5

Warring God, Exodus 15:3, Deuteronomy 21:10

Warrior, Exodus 15:3

Watchtower, Isaiah 21:8

Wedding Garment, Matthew 22:11

Well of Living Water, John 4:11

Whom I Trust, Psalm 144:2

Wisdom of God, Romans 11:33

Wisdom, Psalm 49:3, Psalm 136:5, Ephesians 1:8

With God Is Terrible Majesty, (Terrible means adapted to impress dread, terror or solemn awe, characteristic of God), (Noah Webster, *1828 American Dictionary of the English Language, 10th Edition*, 1998), Job 37:22

Witness, Revelation 1:5

Wonder, Isaiah 29:14

Wonderful Counselor, Isaiah 9:6

Wondrous Gift, Romans 5:18

Word, John 1:1

Word of God, (Sword of the Spirit), Ephesians 6:17, 1 John 1:1, Revelation 19:3

Word of Life, 1 John 1:1

Worthy Is Your Name and You Are Worthy to Be Praised, Ps. 18:3

Worthy to Receive Power, Revelation 5:12

You Are a God that Cannot Be Shaken, Acts 13:17

You Are a God that Does Wonders, Psalm 77:14

You Are a King whose Kingdom Will Have No End,
1 Timothy 1:17, Luke 1:33

You Are a Priest Forever after the Order of Melchizedek,
Psalm 110:4

You Are a Shelter for Me, Psalm 61:3

You Are Anointed with the Oil of Gladness, Psalm 45:7

You Are Exalted Far above All Gods, Psalm 97:9

You Are Exalted High above All Authorities,
1 Chronicles 29:11

You Are Fairer than the Children of Men, Psalm 45:2

You Are from Everlasting to Everlasting, Psalm 90:2

You Are God Alone of All the Kingdoms of the Earth,
Isaiah 37:16

You Are God's Beloved Son, in You God Is Well Pleased,
Luke 3:22

You Are God's Glory, Psalm 45:3

You Are Goodness, Romans 8:28

You Are Harmonious within the Godhead, John 14:26,
Acts 10:38

You Are He that Took Me Out of the Womb, Psalm 22:9

You Are High Above All the Earth, Psalm 97:9

You Are Love, 1 John 3:16

You Are More Glorious and Excellent than the Mountains of
Prey, Psalm 76:4

You Are My All in All, 1 Corinthians 15:28,
Colossians 3:11, Psalm 37:9

You Are My Father, My God, and the Rock of My Salvation, Psalm 89:26

You Are My God from My Conception to My Birth, (from My Mother's Womb), Psalm 22:10

You Are My Hiding Place, Psalm 32:7

You Are My Rock and My Fortress, Psalm 31:3

You Are My Strong Refuge, Psalm 71:7

You Are My Trust from My Youth, Psalm 71:5

You Are of Purer Eyes than to Behold Evil, Habakkuk 1:13

You Are Our Law Giver, Isaiah 33:22

You Are Real, Hebrews 13:8

You Are the Almighty God, Genesis 17:1

You Are the Christ, the Son of the Living God, John 6:69, Matthew 16:16

You are the God of Patience, Psalm 86:15, Ezekiel 33:11, 1 Timothy 2:4, 2 Peter 3:9

You Are the God which Holds My Soul in Life and Does Not Allow My Feet to Be Moved, (He keeps me and surrounds me with protection.), Psalm 66:9

You Are the God which Keeps Covenant and Mercy with Them That Love Him to a Thousand Generations, Deuteronomy 7:9

You Are the God which Made Heaven and Earth, the Sea and All That Is in It, Psalm 146:6

You Are the Helper of the Fatherless, Psalm 10:14

You Are the Same and Your Years Will Not Fail, Hebrews 1:12

You Are the Same, Yesterday and Today and Forever, Hebrew 13:8

You Came from God, the Father, John 16:27

You Care for Me, 1 Peter 5:7

You Care what I Am Going Through, (You See Me), *Holy Bible*, Holman Bible Publisher, Copyright 1985, Crown Reference Edition, Marginal notes, Genesis 16:13

You Do Wondrous Things, Psalm 77:14

You Don't Dwell in Temples Made with Hands, Acts 17:24

You Don't Get Tired of Helping those that Need Help, (You Give Power to the Faint), Isaiah 40:31

You Exalt the Humble, 1 Peter 5:6

You Existed before the Creation, Genesis 1:1-2

You Fill Heaven and Earth, Jeremiah 23:29

You Have a Mighty Arm, Psalm 89:13

You Have Been My Dwelling Place and Will Be in All Generations, Psalm 90:1

You Have Delivered Me from My Bonds of Transgressions and Iniquities, (He has made the bondage of iniquity and sin to be released from me.), Holy Bible, Holman Bible Publisher, Copyright 1985, Crown Reference Edition, Marginal notes, Isaiah 53:5

You Have Delivered My Soul from Death, Psalm 56:13

You Have Dominion from Sea to Sea, and from the River unto the Ends of the Earth, Psalm 72:8

You Have Done Marvelous Things, Psalm 98:1

You Have Given a Banner to Them that Fear You, That It May Be Displayed Because of Truth, Psalm 60:4

You Have Given Me the Heritage of Those that Fear Your Name, Psalm 61:5

You Have Greatness, Psalm 66:3

You Have Made the Heaven and the Earth, Isaiah 45:12

You Have Proved My Heart, Psalm 17:3

You Have Scattered Your Enemies with Your Strong Arm, Psalm 89:10

You Have Tried Me, Psalm 17:3

You Have Visited Me, Psalm 17:3

You Hide Me like a Nursing Mother Keeps Her Nursing Child Close to Her, (El Shaddai), (Thomas E. Ward, *The Names of God*, [Wilmington, DE: Partners in Ministry, 1995] 7-8), Numbers 11:12, Isaiah 66:13

You Know the Number of Hairs on My Head, Matthew 10:30-31

You Know Those that Trust You, Nahum 1:7

You Live Forever and Ever, (Him That Liveth For Ever and Ever),
   Revelation 4:9-10

You Love Righteousness and Hate Wickedness,
   Psalm 45:7

You Made the Worlds, Hebrews 1:2

You Only Are Holy, Revelation 15:4

You Outshine Everyone, Daniel 7:9

You Preserve the Simple, Psalm 116:6

You Publish Peace, (to discover or make known to mankind),
   (Noah Webster, *1828 American Dictionary of the English Language, 10th
   Edition*, 1998), Nahum 1:15

You Reign Over All, 1 Chronicles 29:12

You Rule the Raging of the Sea, Psalm 89:9

You Rule, Judges 8:23

You Save and Regenerate, Titus 3:5

You Save People from Their Sin, Matthew 1:21

You Sit at the Right Hand of God, Hebrews 1:13

You Sit between the Cherubim, Psalm 80:1, Psalm 99:1

You that Destroys the Temple and Builds it in Three Days,
   Mark 15:29

You Understand My Hurts, (You Tell My Wanderings),
   Holy Bible, Holman Bible Publisher, Copyright 1985, Crown Reference
   Edition, Marginal notes, Genesis 16:13, Ps. 56:8

You Were Appointed Heir of All Things, Hebrews 1:2

You Were Planned before the Foundations of the World,
   Galatians 4:4, 5

You Were the Young Child, Having Left Heaven to Become a
   Man. You Were Sent as a King to Deliver Me, Matthew 2:8,
   Luke 1:31-33

You Will Be Revealed from Heaven with Your Mighty Angels, in
   Flaming Fire, 2 Thessalonians 1:7

You Will Endure Forever and Ever, Psalm 102:12

You Will Judge Your People, Hebrews 10:30

You, LORD, Are High Above All the Earth, Psalm 97:9

You, O LORD, Are Our Father, Our Redeemer, Isaiah 63:16

Your Glory, and Majesty, Psalm 45:3

Your Compassion Does Not Fail, Lamentation 3:22

Your Dominion Endures Throughout All Generations, Psalm 145:13

Your Elect in Whom You Delight, Isaiah 42:1

Your Holy Mountain, Isaiah 65:11

Your Lovingkindness Is Better than Life, Psalm 63:3

Your Name Is Excellent, Psalm 8:1

Your Name Is from Everlasting, Isaiah 63:16

Your Name Is Good, Psalm 54:6

Your Right Hand Is Full of Righteousness, Psalm 48:10

Your Right Hand Upholds Me, Psalm 63:8

Your Right Hand, O LORD, Is Become Glorious in Power, Exodus 15:6

Your Son Jesus, Acts 3:26

Your Throne Is Established of Old and You Are from Everlasting, Psalm 93:2

Your Throne Is Righteousness and Judgment, Psalm 97:2

Your Understanding Is Infinite, Psalm 119:130

Zealous, (Passion for God's House burns within Me), Numbers 25:13, John 2:17

Bible verses that describe the manifold beauty of God:

Alpha, Omega, Beginning, Ending, Is, Was And Which Is To Come, The Almighty, Revelation 1:8

Alpha, Omega, First, Last, Revelation 1:11

Brought Us Out Of Egypt, Psalm 81:1

Builds Up Jerusalem, Gathers Together The Outcasts Of Israel, Heals The Broken In Heart, Binds Up Their Wounds, Tells The Number Of The Stars And Calls Them All By Their Names, Great Power, Understanding Is Infinite, Lifts The Humble, Casts Down The Wicked, Covers The Heaven With Clouds, Prepares Rain For The Earth, Makes Grass To Grow On The Mountains, Gives The Animals Food, Takes Pleasure In The People That Fear Him And In Those That Hope In His Mercy, Fills Us With His Word, Sends His Commandment Upon Earth, His Word Runs Quickly, Makes Snow And Ice, He Shows His Word Unto Jacob, Psalm 147:1-20

Defense, Rock, Refuge, Psalm 94:22

Description Of Ancient Of Day's Appearance And His Throne, Daniel 7:9

Description Of The King Of Kings And LORD Of Lords, Revelation 19:1, 2, 6, 11-12, 15-16

Does Wonders And Declares His Strength To People, Psalm 77:13, 14

Dwells Between The Cherubim, Is God, Made Heavens And Earth, Psalm 80:1

Exalted For His Strength, Psalm 21:13

Exercises Lovingkindness, Judgment And Righteousness,
Jeremiah 9:24

From Everlasting Even Before The Mountains And The
Earth's Formation, Psalms 90:2

From Jesse's Root A Branch Will Grow, With The Spirit Of
The LORD Resting Upon Him, The Spirit Of Wisdom
And Understanding, The Spirit Of Counsel And Might,
The Spirit Of Knowledge And Of The Fear Of The LORD,
With Quick Understanding, Judging Not After The
Vision Of The Eyes Or The Hearing Of The Ears But In
Righteousness Judging The Poor, Reproving With
Equity For The Meek Of The Earth, Faithful,
Isaiah 11:1-5

God Of Jacob Is My Help, Hope Is In The Lord Which Made
Heaven, Earth And Sea, Keeps Truth Forever, Executes
Judgment For The Oppressed, Feeds The Hungry, Lets
Prisoners Go, Opens The Eyes Of The Blind, Raises Up
Those That Are Humbled, Loves The Righteous,
Preserves Those In Need, Relieves The Fatherless And
Widow, Turns The Wicked Upside Down, Reigns Forever
Unto All Generations, Psalm 146:5-10

Great And Solemn Name Which Is Holy, Psalm 99:3

Great Merciful Kindness, Truth Lasts Forever,
Psalm 117:2

Great Works, Deep Thoughts, High Forever,
Psalm 92:5, 8

Has Done Faithful Things, Counsels Are Faithfulness And
Truth, Strength To The Poor, Strength To The Needy In
Distress, Refuge From The Storm, Shadow From The
Heat, Isaiah 25:1, 4

Has Done Marvelous Things, His Right Hand And His Holy
Arm Gave Him The Victory, Psalm 98:1

He Is Holy True, He Has the Key of David, He Opens, He Shuts, Revelation 3:7

High Above All Nations, Glory Above The Heavens, Dwells On High, Humbles Himself To See Things In Heaven And Earth, Psalms 113:4-6

High Above All The Earth, Exalted Far Above All Gods, Psalm 97:9

High And Elevated One Inhabiting Eternity, Whose Name Is Holy, Dwells In The High And Holy Place With Those That Have A Humble Spirit To Revive The Heart Of The Humble, Isaiah 57:15

High And Lifted Up, Holy Lord, Seraphim Around Him, Isaiah 6:1-3

His Name Is Holy And Reverend, Psalm 111:9

Hope And Youthful Trust, Psalm 71:5

I AM THAT I AM, Exodus 3:14

JEHOVAH, Most High Over All The Earth, Psalm 83:18

Jesus Christ Forever The Same, Hebrews 13:8

Jesus Is The Christ, Son Of Man Sits On The Right Hand Of God, Coming In The Clouds Of Heaven, Keeps Us From Sinning, Presents Us Faultless Before The Presence Of His Glory With Great Joy, Only Wise God, Savior, Dominion, Power,
Jude 24-25

Laid The Foundation Of The Earth, Heavens Are The Work Of His Hands, Psalm 102:25

Lives Though Was Dead, Alive Forevermore, Has The Keys Of Hell And Of Death, Revelation 1:18

Major Part Of His Character, Exodus 34:6-7

Mercy Is Great Above Heaven, Truth Reaches unto the Clouds, Psalm 108:4

Might Of His Presence In Heaven, Who Is Around Him In

Heaven, What They Look Like, What They Say, Revelation 4:3-11

My Inheritance, Psalm 16:5

Name Alone Is Excellent, Glory Is above the Earth and Heaven, Psalm 148:13

No Other God So Great As Our God, Psalm 77:13

Omniscient, Omnipotent, Manifold Wisdom, Ecclesiastes 3:14-15

Perfect And Right, Deuteronomy 32:4

Physical Appearance Of Jesus Christ In Heaven, How His Voice Sounds, Right Hand Has Seven Stars, Out Of His Mouth A Sharp Two-Edged Sword, Appearance of His Countenance, Revelation 1:13-16

Priest For Ever After The Order Of Melchizedek, Psalm 110:4

Puts Those Who Are Alone Into Families And Releases People Out Of Chains, Psalm 68:6

Refuge, Strength, Help In Trouble, Psalm 46:1

Rock and Redeemer, Psalm 78:35

Rides Upon The Heavens, Deuteronomy 33:26

Sanctuary, Stone Of Stumbling, Rock Of Offense To Both Houses Of Israel, Snare To The Inhabitants Of Jerusalem, Isaiah 8:14

Sign Of The Son Of Man In Heaven As He Comes In Clouds Of Heaven And The Response From Those On Earth, Matthew 24:30

Son Of Man Sits On The Right Hand Of God, Comes In The Clouds Of Heaven, Matthew 26:64

Spirit Of The Lord God Is On Him, Anointed To Preach Good News To The Meek, Heals The Brokenhearted, Proclaims Liberty To The Captives, Opens Those Bound In Prison, Proclaims The Year Of The Lord, God Will Be

The Avenger, Comforts Those That Are Sad, Gives
Beauty For Ashes, Oil Of Joy To Those That Mourn,
Praise To Those Heavy In Spirit That He Might Be
Glorified,
Isaiah 61:1-3

Stone The Builders Refused, Became The Head Stone Of
The Corner, Psalm 118:22

Strength Of My Salvation, Protects Me In Battle,
Psalm 140:7

Strong Tower, Safe, Proverbs 18:10

Terrible, (Adapted To Impress Dread, Terror Or Solemn Awe),
And A Great King Over All The Earth,
Psalm 47:2

The God Of All Eternity That Reigns, Revelation 11:17

The Same And Years Have No End, Psalm 102:27

View Under His Feet, Exodus 24:10

What Are The Praises To Jesus Christ In Heaven,
Revelation 7:12

Worthy To Take The Book And To Open The Seals Of It
Because He Was Slain, He Makes Us Kings And Priests,
The Lamb's Worthiness,
R 5:9, 10, 12

Michelle Holstein lives in rural Iowa and enjoys the simple things in life. As a student of the Word of God, she is passionate about how God Almighty has faithfully revealed Himself to mankind. She enjoys learning about the character of God.

Because of the trials in her life, she has found solace and comfort in the presence of God and knows that He is our answer in any situation. As an exhorter, she has endeavored to share her victories with others.

Michelle hopes that you will read and apply this book and her other "10 Minutes" books as tools to further enhance your devotional time each day.

Website: www.HolsteinBooks.com

Email: HolsteinBooks@gmail.com

 **michelle.holstein.372**

Other books in this series are:

10 Minutes of Prayer with Scriptures to Grow Faith

10 Minutes of Promise with the Rock of Ages

10 Minutes of Pursuit when Loneliness Strikes

Made in the USA
Columbia, SC
21 September 2020